Honolulu
HAWAII
PACIFIC OCEAN
EQUATOR
PHOENIX IS.
MARQUESAS IS.
S.
SAMOA
Apia
SOCIETY IS.
Tahiti
COOK IS.
ONGA
Nuku'alofa
Tropic of Capricorn
AF251012

Fiji Islands

Fiji Islands

Hank Curth

WITH TEXT BY SUE WENDT

NELSON

To the people of Fiji

THOMAS NELSON (AUSTRALIA) LIMITED
597 Little Collins Street Melbourne 3000
403 George Street Sydney 2000

THOMAS NELSON AND SONS LTD
36 Park Street London W1Y 4DE

THOMAS NELSON AND SONS
(SOUTH AFRICA) PTY LTD
PO Box 7331 Johannesburg

THOMAS NELSON AND SONS (CANADA) LTD
81 Curlew Drive Don Mills Ontario

SBN 17 001920 9

Printed in Hong Kong
by Toppan Printing Co Ltd

Photographic Data

For all the photographs in this book I used three Asahi Pentax Spotmatic bodies, one of which is fitted with a motor drive, and a range of lenses including
17mm F4 Fisheye Takumar,
28mm F3.5 Super Takumar,
35mm F2 Super Takumar,
50mm F1.4 Super Takumar,
50mm F4 Macro Takumar,
105mm F2.8 Super Takumar,
135mm F3.5 Super Takumar,
70/150mm F4.5 Super Takumar Zoom,
200mm F4 Super Takumar.

In addition to the built-in meters of the Spotmatic bodies, I occasionally used an Asahi Pentax Spotmeter. Marine shots were photographed with a Nikonos II 35mm underwater camera.
All cameras and lenses were carried in water-tight aluminium cases lined with foam shock-absorbing material, which also kept heat and humidity from the equipment.
Films used were Kodachrome II and High Speed Ektachrome for colour; Kodak Tri-X for black and white.
Research and interviews on location were recorded on an Akai XV portable stereo recorder.

Acknowledgements

The idea for this book was born out of the desire to tell the story of the Fiji Islands through the eyes of the twentieth century traveller. As no two people ever view a locale with the same perception or emotions, there must be omissions, but an honest effort has been made to give an overall view of these once remote islands.
The kindness and generosity of the men, women and children of the Fiji Islands will for ever be embedded deeply in our hearts.
The unselfish and generous support of the following organisations who, without restriction or thought of publicity for themselves, backed this work wholeheartedly, is acknowledged.

Avis Rent A Car System Pty Ltd, Bank of New South Wales, British Overseas Airways Corporation, Brown Marine Ltd, Burns Philp (South Sea) Co. Ltd, Carnes Jannif Ltd, Fiji Airways, Fiji Government Departments (Agriculture and Botany, Bureau of Statistics, Philatelic Bureau and Public Relations Office), Fiji Museum, Fiji Visitors Bureau, Korolevu Beach Hotel, Mocambo Hotel, South Sea Lands Ltd, Stinsons Ltd, The Fijian Yanuca Island Resort, *The Fiji Times*, Travelodge Fiji Ltd.

The following sources were consulted in the preparation of the text: *A History of Fiji*, R. A. Derrick, *The Fiji Islands*, R. A. Derrick, *With Hook, Line and Snorkel in the South Pacific*, R. Wright, *King of the Cannibal Isles*, A. B. Brewster, *Handbook of Fiji*, J. Tudor (ed), Pacific Publications, *Fiji Times* Centennial Supplement, *Fiji Times*, *The Charter of the Land*, Peter France, *A Field Guide to Fiji Birds*, Robin Mercer.

We also would like to pay tribute and express our thanks to the many individuals throughout the islands, from Government ministers to plantation workers, from village chiefs to shopkeepers, who assisted us so enthusiastically . . . and special thanks to Bob and Annette Hunter.

SUF WENDT   HANK CURTH

Contents

Foreword

By Bruce Palmer, B.A., Dip. Tchg., Director of the Fiji Museum, Suva.

In this era of jet-stop itineraries it is easy to claim for the islands of Fiji the status of international cross-roads, as if, perhaps, by manipulating timetables and air-miles, travel agents and carriers had between them created for Fiji a new and critical role in South Pacific transport. One would not deny the status claimed; Fiji certainly is a cross-roads with a radiating network of island links that one would expect of such a centre. Its role, however, is the product of more ancient times, of men and women who did not know the intricacies of aircraft, ocean liners or map-making.

For a period of three thousand years before the advent of flying, unknown voyagers were crossing the seas, making landfalls behind the reef and leaving their imprint in the sands fringing the bush. They were the true pioneers of travel, maritime people whose daring and seamanship made Fiji a cross-roads in antiquity. Over these shores have passed many canoe crews, some to stay and others to set off at some later date for other isles in other latitudes.

This is the appeal of Fiji: one feels a sense of continuity in the prehistoric blending of peoples and cultures now carried on more rapidly by new ethnic sources unknown in the past. By plane and ship new arrivals are making their own individual discoveries and finding a sense of adventure in doing it. For discovery and adventure can be experienced in Fiji, not just in the coral beaches of a strangely named or shaped island, or in mountains where rocky bluffs frown on the river traveller, but in the field of human relations too. The latter could be the more significant, for beaches and bluffs are universal, or nearly so, but cultural crucibles are rarer. One can easily enough see isolated elements wherever the jet-stop may be, or elsewhere see the completed amalgam. To experience separate elements each in their own state and also in the process of compatible adjustment is an adventure and a discovery in human relationships.

This process of growth against a backdrop of varied tropic beauty is typical of Fiji. There is something to interest and excite even the most phlegmatic character stepping onto Fiji soil for the first time.

This book will help some readers to make armchair explorations and perhaps stimulate them to experience the reality of it all. Others will recall the joys of itinerant escapists from the concrete and glass of an urban existence. To others again it will be a glimpse of their home, a friendly island world.

The Islands

Spelling and Pronunciation

In this book the local spelling of Fijian words, including place names, is used. The pronunciation can be a little confusing. People arriving by air, for instance, find it hard to understand why the name of the airport is pronounced 'Nandi' when it is spelled 'Nadi' The following pronunciation peculiarities will help a little.

b is pronounced *mb* as in timber
c is pronounced *th* as in thy
d is pronounced *nd* as in handy
g is pronounced *ng* as in singer
q is pronounced *ng* as in finger.

Population

At the end of 1969 the population of Fiji, including Rotuma, reached 527,000.

Population distribution is made up as follows:

Fijian	220,000
Indian	263,000
European	14,000
Part-European	10,000
Chinese	5,000
Other Pacific races	15,000

Trade figures 1969

Imports	$77,888,000
Exports	$43,548,000
Re-exports	$9,679,000

Industries in order of importance

1 Sugar
316,000 tons ($28,134,000)
2 Tourism
$26,000,000
3 Coconut Oil
17,000 tons ($3,909,000)
4 Gold
95,000 fine ozs ($3,361,000)
5 Seed cake, coconut meal
8,000 tons ($384,000)
6 Copra
1,000 tons ($249,000)

What are they, these islands of Fiji, these green and golden specks of land flung at random on a southern sea? As close as a jet's journey from any corner of the earth, as elusive as the history their people never knew how to write, the Fiji Isles are many things. To many people.

The transient observer sees only the surge and colour of the market place, translucent seas glittering under a tropic sun, coconut palms feathering and swaying to the gentle touch of the tradewinds. Hibiscus flowers bloom pink and brazen red and the Fijian people smile and make you feel that theirs is true, uncalculated friendliness. For the visitor, Fiji is coral islands, sun-drenched, palm-fringed, idyllic places, needing no words to enhance their appeal. It is copra plantations, sweeping cane fields, mountains of sugar ready for bagging and loading for export. There are many faces of Fiji, faces harder to define. They have an illusory quality, as mysterious to the outsider as the ageless rites of Melanesian witchcraft and as difficult to grasp as the many meanings of Fiji's different dialects.

There is romance and industry here, myth and materialism, mystique and pragmatism. There is enormous optimism—and booming investment. Politics are not new to the islands, but here they have a strength and vigour that ensures that Fiji will always be a leader in South Pacific affairs. Yet Fiji resembles a halfway house still, precariously poised between what used to be and what must inevitably come. Part of it remains in the last century, rooted in the minds of people who still believe in devilry and witchcraft. The rest is progres-

Left:
Evening, Suva Harbour

Right:
The Navua River delta with Beqa Island in
the distance

sing as fast as the growing number of locally-born, overseas-trained professional men and educationists can push it ahead.

Although spread across 250,000 square miles of the south-west portion of the Pacific Ocean, still within the steamy tropics but slipping southwards, the land area of the Fiji Group totals only 7,055 square miles. A little over eighty per cent of this is Fijian communal land; the rest is Crown and freehold land, the latter much sought after by investors. Land prices have soared in recent years and the boom in real estate is hand in hand with the boom in tourism. The largest of the Fiji islands is Viti Levu (meaning 'Great Fiji') with an area of 4,011 square miles. This is the most heavily populated island and Suva, the capital, is located along its south-east coast. Second largest is Vanua Levu ('Great Land') 2,137 square miles and thick with copra plantations and planters' traditions. The bulk of Vanua Levu's population centres around the sugar town of Labasa and the hot little port of Savusavu, both of which have airports and regular air services. Almost a century ago, a farsighted resident urged the populace to publicise Savusavu's hot springs—'let us catch some tourists and bathe them'—its mild climate and good fishing, but only in the late 60s did the town succumb to planned tourist development.

Taveuni, twenty-six miles long and seven miles wide, ranks next in size. This 'Garden of Fiji', so named because of its rich soils and lush and varied vegetation, is also the source of an astonishing variety of ghost stories. Kadavu, the first landmark sighted by voyagers from the

Left: BOAC VC10, Nadi International Airport

Right: Tourists crowd the decks, Suva Harbour

south, is the fourth largest island—158 square miles—and then come all the dots on the map that constitute this fragmented land, including the mystical island of Bau, home of the High Chiefs and historically important Ovalau, where the one-time capital of Fiji, Levuka, now slumbers amid its memories of yesterday's glory.

There is always confusion about the actual number of fragments, for it depends upon one's own interpretation. The Fiji Visitors' Bureau has energetically promoted Fiji's '300 Islands in the Sun', but if one counts

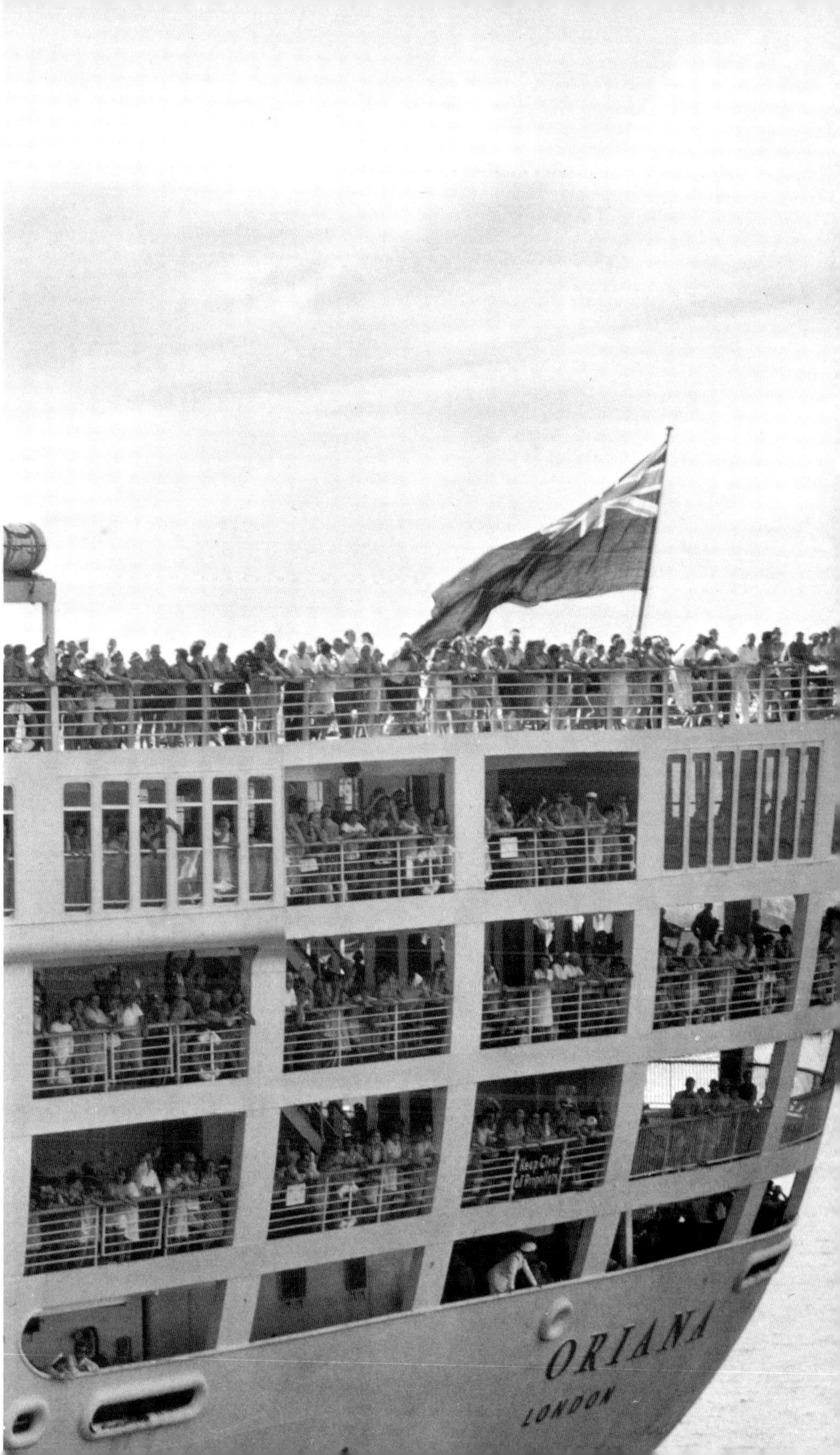

South eastern coast, Vanua Levu

the numerous wooded rocks and sand-cays and nameless islets, the total is closer to 800. There are 300 with an area of more than one square mile and a hundred of these are permanently inhabited. Most islands in the archipelago are either completely volcanic in formation, having been thrust above the surface of the sea by some impossibly distant cataclysmic happening, or they are a composite of volcanic and limestone formation.

Varying climatic conditions create a panoramic paint-box of enormous contrast, from the harsh yellow-

Vatu Vara, or Hat Island, sighted and described by Lieut. William Bligh, captain of HMS *Providence* on his second voyage to Fiji in 1791

browns and primary greens of the dry zones to the lush rain-forest verdure of the wet. There are hills and crags and jagged mountain ranges, vast tracts of creeping mangrove swamp, jungle-smothered valleys of vine and parasitic growth, waterfalls and limpid pools, stretching plains and fertile river flats. This scattered land sees violent tropical storms and, sometimes, hurricanes. It experiences months of drought, when cane crops wither and rivers dwindle to a sluggish stream, but it is in the clement seasons, when nights are balmy and heavy with that almost tangible scent of the tropics, that Fiji comes close to lomalagi—or paradise.

The main island of Viti Levu, third largest in the open Pacific and only slightly smaller than Hawaii, has all these variations. With the path to the dry north-west barred by a central spine of mountains, the prevailing winds drop their rains on the windward slopes, to be absorbed by voracious rain-forest and jungle vegetation. The division between this 'wet' zone and the open grasslands of the 'dry' is easily discernible from the air. It is a reminder that here is a country of contradiction, a country where lush growth lives side by side with sparse, flood with drought, rich with poor. And a reminder, perhaps, that this element of contrast, inherent in Fiji's nature, has had a profound effect in the human sphere, for there must be more anomalies and contradictions among the polyglot population of this small land than in any other country of comparable size and population.

In the wet zone, on the Suva side, the residents wilt in the blanket-thick moistness of the humid December to March summer months,

envying hotel guests their air conditioned comforts and coveting the dryer heat of the Nadi side of Viti Levu. The capital city receives 120 inches of torrentially delivered rain a year, most of it falling in short-lived bursts, flooding the streets and bringing forth vast armies of frogs and toads to squat stolidly on footpaths and sodden lawns. One sometimes feels as though delicate webs are about to form between one's own fingers and toes. On its fine days, Suva is a pleasing metropolis of clean, tree-shaded streets, carefully-tended tropical gardens, plush hotels and poky little duty free stores. Its broad, deep harbour, set against a backdrop of thickly wooded mountains, is the focal point of this cosmopolitan centre that they call the hub of the South Pacific. On the one side stands the remainder of a long-gone volcano, a thumb-like peak appropriately called Joske's Thumb. Lining the foreshore on the other are mini-skyscrapers which conceal behind them, like the facade of a film-set, a confusion of architectural styles representing the Melanesian, Polynesian, Indian and old Colonial influences that have helped to shape today's Fiji. Although a hepped-up traffic system belies the traditional somnolence of the tropics, the city still retains just enough South Seas languor to frustrate, charm, amuse or irritate businessmen who want to get things done in a hurry. The pace of daily life in Suva is fast enough to widen the eyes of villagers and 'bush' Fijians who come in on week-end jaunts, but not fast enough to be conducive to ulcers.

Left:
Yanuca Island resort, Viti Levu
Right: Plantation, Mago Island, Lau Group

Contemporary Fijian Balabala or tree-fern carving

The almost constant blue skies of the dry west, the Nadi side, help stoke the friendly rivalry between Suva and the international airport town. Each boasts duty-free stores, bustling market-places, hospitable people, good accommodation. Suva offers more entertainment and an excellent harbour; Nadi has an international airport and the better climate. Linking the two is the hotel and resort-studded strip of white beach and clear water known as the Coral Coast, a tourist playground that manages to escape being either tawdry or over-priced, although

The chiefly island of Serua near Korolevu

catering for thousands. Holiday on the Coral Coast and you still manage to be away from it all, for there are miles of beach where you'll not see a soul except perhaps a lone Fijian fisherman, or a group of Fijian *maramas* trudging home with the day's spoils. In the Sabeto Valley and along the banks of the Sigatoka River, roughly midway between Nadi and Suva, are Viti Levu's richest pastures, patchwork fields of maize, water-melons, tobacco, passion-fruit, rice, sugar-cane and root vegetables. From Lautoka to Ba and right through to Rakiraki on the north-east lip, stretches Viti Levu's sugar-cane country, acres and acres of cane fanning out in every direction, the backbone of the economy and the heart of many of Fiji's political polemics.

Scattered throughout the archipelago like nature's jewels are the coral islands, the isles of travellers' dreams and picture postcards, inspiration for poetry, poetic in themselves. Seen from above, they float in a blue that robs the sky of colour, a vast and deliquescent tapestry that is never only blue but sometimes jade, sometimes emerald, sometimes glimmering, shimmering turquoise. To wander along the white sands of these atolls is to relive, with a shock, memories of childhood fantasies that seemed so real yet remained, always, other-worldly . . . here they are and you can't quite believe them. Yet the beauty of these palm-studded atolls is a superficial thing, for they are of little economic value. They are bereft of hills and streams and atoll dwellers must live on an unending diet of coconuts and fish, healthy but monotonous.

Tropical rainforest, Nausori Highlands *(top)*;
Sabeto Valley near Nadi at dawn *(centre)*;
dunes at the mouth of Sigatoka river
(bottom); mountain ranges in the dry-zone
of Viti Levu near Nadi *(right)*

Weaving an intricate, potentially treacherous, maze of seaways throughout all the Fiji islands are the coral reefs, thousands of miles of them, built up over centuries by countless billions of primitive living creatures called polyps. Building and dying and building, feeding on the animal plankton floating in the surface layers of the ocean, these minute, mindless creatures have entombed themselves into monumental coral masses which now support a phantasmagoric wonderland of animal and vegetable life. By forming protective coral girdles around almost all of Fiji's islands, the reefs provide rich fishing grounds from which the islanders, using unique and ancient methods, gather great quantities of their native foods—beche-de-mer, seaweeds, molluscs and marine fish. But for the unsuspecting seafarer the reefs are a maze of trouble, and since the coming of the first European voyager, Fiji waters have been a graveyard for ships. Now and then, when flying over the Group, one sees sunlight glinting on a reef-stranded hulk, as it rides out the months until wind and waves complete the destruction.

The longest single reef in Fiji is the Great Sea Reef, stretching 300 miles from south-west Viti Levu to the north of neighbouring Vanua Levu. Many fishing vessels have ended their days decorating the coral outcrops guarding the entrance passage into Suva Harbour, for while the harbour itself is safe for ships of any size, manoeuvring them through the barrier reef requires experience and skill.

Least visited and least documented of Fiji's islands are those of the far-flung Lau Group, strung away to the

east and closer to Tonga than they
are to Viti Levu and its capital city,
Suva. The names roll off the tongue
like syrup, names like Cicia, Wai-
lagilala, Mago, Kanacea, Kabara,
Ono-i-Lau, Moce, Tuvuca. Dis-
persed over 44,000 square miles of
ocean, the Laus are so far removed
from each other that they seem per-
petually wreathed in the purple mists
of distance. Adding to the air of
mystery is the fact that relatively few
people can quote statistics about
Lau. You feel you're the first to tread
those gracefully curving beaches—
and the spontaneous excitement of

Sugar cane fields near Nadi

the local populace as you clamber ashore from some visiting ship's punt shows that not too many similarly adventuring feet have paved the way.

The Lau Group is rich in both Fijian and Tongan history; links with the past are strong. There is a village called Lomaloma, on the island of Vanua Balavu, where traditional Tongan action songs and dances are performed by people as Tongan in character and appearance as those who braved the unknown to voyage there with the great Tongan chief, Ma'afu, in the middle of last century. The results of Polynesian migrations to these parts can be seen in the facial features and lighter skin of the Lauan people.

Administrative centre of the Lau Group is Tubou village, on the island of Lakeba, where the first Wesleyan missionaries settled in 1835. Today Tubou is a delightful oasis in the middle of nowhere, a collection of neatly-kept cottages and elaborate bures, smooth village greens where cricket is played in the English tradition, productive vegetable patches and devout Fijians dressing in their Sunday best to attend services at the

Survey beacon, Taveuni Island

Rabi Island off Vanua Levu

historic church. Here, too, are the burial grounds of men who helped mould Fiji: Prince Ma'afu, Ratu Tevita Uluilakeba and the great Fijian statesman, Ratu Sir Lala Sukuna. Their white-painted tombs, lovingly decorated with plastic domes filled with flowers, are set apart in a grassy mound, watched over by a solitary coconut palm.

Decades may pass before Lau succumbs to what some consider the corrupting effects of tourism— though the people themselves are eager for all the accoutrements of progress. This skein of copra-rich islands is too remote to be spoiled easily by brash new hotels and sprawling holiday resorts, even though this very remoteness is the main attraction for visitors.

The rock settings and elaborate headstones of ancient burial grounds dominate the landscape on Rotuma, 330 miles north of Nadi. Rotumans revered their dead with an almost Oriental intensity and in the old days it was customary for relatives of a dead person to build a temporary shelter so that they might live on or near the grave for some time after the death.

A part of Fiji, yet somehow apart from Fiji's affairs, Rotuma has not been eager for headlong progress or a tide of tourists. The people preferred to send those young ones seeking change to the outside world rather than encourage the outside world to encroach upon their own peaceful existence. Their compact island, small enough to drive around in a couple of hours, produces some of the best oranges in the Pacific, and magnificent yams, tapioca and tropical fruits. Also isolated from the affairs of Fiji, but subject to its laws, are the islands of Kioa and Rabi,

both owned by foreign communities. The Ellice Islanders of Kioa are reticent and keep much to themselves, but the 2,000 and more Banabans of Rabi have been vociferous in their requests for more of the phosphate income from Ocean Island, their original home in the Gilbert and Ellice Island Group. In 1968 they sent a telegram to the Queen of England about it, even took their case to the British Government. But they were advised finally to be satisfied with fertile Rabi and a proportion of Ocean Island's phosphate returns.

Because it straddles the 180th meridian, which was also the International Date Line, Fiji has a head start on the rest of the world. The meridian slices through the Moala Group and across the Koro Sea, through Taveuni, Rabi and the eastern end of Vanua Levu. In the early days of Fiji's settlement by *vavalagi* (the Fijian word for white foreigners, meaning, strictly, 'Comers from the Heavens') there were numerous stories about the difficulties of living astride the date line, half in today and half in tomorrow. One half of a man's property might be in Saturday, when all manner of festivities were allowed, and the other in Sunday, which had to be observed with true Christian piety. There's the story of the shopkeeper who conducted business through the front door for six days of the week and through the back door, where it was still Saturday, on the seventh. The solution to such a schizophrenic situation was to 'bend' the line a little, so that it ran between Tonga and Samoa. The Fiji Islands now have a uniform time, twelve hours ahead of Greenwich Mean Time.

Land

Because Fiji has only 447,000 acres of land which is classified as freehold and therefore can be bought and sold freely, land values have soared in recent years. The local populace has watched, amazed, as overseas investors have paid what are, by Fiji standards, staggering sums for islands and beach frontages for tourist developments. No new freehold land can be created, except as a result of sale or exchange of Crown land.

The Crown owns 87,000 acres of freehold land plus a further 85,000 acres of land declared vacant by the Native Lands Commission and 148,000 acres of Fijian land the owning units of which have become extinct. Crown freehold may not be sold except in very special circumstances, but it can be leased.

Tribal land belonging to Fijians totals 3,747,000 acres, owned communally by more than 6,500 recognised land owning units. Tribal land, which cannot be sold, is administered by the Native Land Trust Board.

After the needs of the Fijian landowners are met, remaining land is made available for leasing In recent years, when hotel or tourist resort developers have sought land, the Board has fixed terms ensuring the Fijian owners a participation in the profits.

Industries

Sugar, gold and coconuts have long been the three major industries of Fiji, but tourism must now be counted in the forefront of the island's money-earners.

Fiji's secondary industries were based until recently on the processing of agricultural products. But here, too, the field has been widened and Fiji now produces an astonishing variety of products both for home consumption and export. Even the kai shellfish and 'lolo', the coconut cream in which so many Fijian dishes are cooked, are now canned in a Suva factory and exported.

The fast-expanding range of products now being produced in Fiji includes aluminium products, barbed wire, batteries, beer, biscuits, boats, brooms, butter, candles, cement, ceiling installations, cigarettes, clothing, concrete products and ready-mixed concrete, coconut products, confectionery, cordials and mineral waters, cultured pearls, fibreglass products, fibrous plaster products, fish meal, fruit and vegetable juices and pulp, furniture, handicrafts, honey, jewellery, ice cream, industrial gases, matches, meat preparations, metal containers, nails, paints, paper products, perfumery products, plastics, plywood, poultry feeds, roll-formed iron roofing, tobacco, flip-flops, sauces, wrought-iron products and ready-made garments.

In addition there is a fisheries base and freezing plant, rice milling, bauxite, copper and manganese mining, and a number of servicing industries including dry-cleaning, laundering, tyre retreading, electroplating, radio repairing, motor vehicle repairing and body building, printing, including silk screen printing, upholstering, general engineering, civil engineering and building and marine engineering, slipway management, real estate and advertising agencies, commercial colour film processing and data processing by computer system.

Suva has three slipways, can take vessels up to 1,000 tons and has ship-building and repair firms.

People

Sweet stall, Sigatoka

To mingle with the boisterous, exuberant onlookers at a big sporting match, or at one of the gay multi-purpose festivals of Fiji, is to realise that these islands can no longer be identified by a single race. Joined in the pursuit of enjoyment the polyglot population becomes a many-coloured canvas of Fijian, Indian, Chinese, European, part-European, Rotuman and Polynesian faces, unlike of feature though united in appreciating simple pleasures. Each speaks his different language, even his different dialect. Each thinks his different thoughts, follows his different customs and worships his different god.

In this multi-racial society of more than half a million people the Indians, relative newcomers, outnumber the indigenous Fijians. They contribute an essential part of the atmosphere and vitality that is to-day's Fiji. In the barter of the market-place a black-braided Hindu girl, unable to read or write but shrewd beyond her years, haggles with a tourist while her grandmother, wrapped wraith-like in white, sits nearby with thoughts turned inward and a gold ornament glinting in her nostril. In the Legislative Council a Gujerati lawyer, his profession learned in an Australian university, propounds his political theories in English faintly tinged with the sing-song influence of his native tongue. In the temple on the hill, a Sikh priest in turban and spotless dhoti, sits cross-legged beneath a picture of a handprint—the handprint of Guru Nanak, founder of the Sikh religion. Beneath the icing-sugar domes and graceful spires of the Muslim mosque at Toorak, devotees bow low and pray to Allah six times a day. There are surgeons, dentists,

Colourful open-air buses are still
fashionable

scores of lawyers. Tailors toil before
row upon row of old-fashioned sew-
ing machines. Their women, with
their passion for vivid pinks and
purple, dazzling yellow and iridescent green, make a rainbow pattern
of colour in the streets and in the
cane fields. They are people remote
from this corner of the South Seas,
yet an integral part of it.

The role of the European, who has made his mark indelibly in government, in technological fields, education and administration, is a complex one, for with whole-scale localisation of the country's affairs, there is no place now for the small army of expatriates who used to fill government houses and government positions and go 'back home' on fare-paid overseas leave every three or four years. Some of the best-known and longest-established names in Fiji belong to the part-Europeans, descendants of the male settlers who arrived here and took wives from amongst the local Fijians, Tongans and other Islanders. They now make up about two per cent of the population and although, like mixed-bloods everywhere, they sometimes have a 'neither here nor there' feeling, they have the advantage in Fiji of being able to experience the best of both worlds.

Yet another sphere is the Chinese community, quiet, law-abiding, its members taking part in almost every aspect of daily commerce without fuss or fanfare. Frugal and hard-working, they first came to Fiji as free settlers in the days when im-migration was unrestricted, and took their place in the Colony as merchants, shop-keepers, market gardeners and tradesmen. Their restaurants are popular with locals of all nationalities, including the Rotumans, the Tongans the Samo-ans, the Gilbertese and all the other Islanders who have made Fiji their home.

But amidst this hotch-potch popula-tion, it is the Fijian, only now begin-ning to develop any real business acumen, who still owns the land. The world thinks of him as being the carefree, careless and friendly Melanesian described by a thousand smitten travel writers in a thousand eulogies. This modern Melanesian, with his Polynesian admixture, is not the same breed as the blood-thirsty ancestor who earned his homeland the unhappy title, Cannibal Isles. He is certainly friendly, almost over-whelmingly hospitable, but he is neither carefree nor careless. Fijians are too much torn between two worlds to be free of care or careless of the future. Beneath that happy, handsome exterior they are develop-ing a strong nationalism and a fierce determination to guide their own

Saturday morning market, Sigatoka

Right:
Money changes—time changes. Former shipboard bankers are now airborne visiting the outer islands

fate. Their path isn't easy. The University of the South Pacific is at Suva —yet only a very small proportion of Fijian children have so far reached secondary school. Little more than a century ago, none of them went to school at all, so small wonder if they are not as wise in the ways of the world or as familiar with a materialistic society as the Indians, Europeans and Chinese of Fiji. Fijian children are just as bright as any other group of youngsters—but both they and their parents have had a lot of catching up to do. Money, for one thing, has been a new con-

cept of wealth for them.

In the old days it was food that measured a man's affluence and so long as he had ample dalo and yam, good fishing grounds and the omnipresent coconut, he was never wanting. Now he finds himself in competition with races who've had centuries of experience with a money economy. It has made him a Jack-of-all-trades in a time when he hasn't really had a chance to become master of any. The growth of tourism—which vies with sugar as Fiji's main revenue-earner—has done much to complicate the de-

46

BANK OF NEW SOUTH WALES
M.V. "RATANUI" AGENCY

ceptively simple Fijian formula for living, for with much of the coastal fringe of Viti Levu and some of the outer islands studded with hotels and beach-side resorts, thousands of Fijians and Indians have found new and unfamiliar forms of employment. The Indians tend to tackle these jobs with seriousness and a fair degree of application, the Fijians, with rather less of both . . . but an enormous amount of good humour. Visitors love to relate incidents experienced in Fiji hotels, some of them quite unbelievable, even when true. There was the waiter who smiled knowledgeably when asked for the vodka and orange cocktail known as a Screwdriver. He departed for a lengthy period—and returned with the carpenters' tool of the same name placed proudly in the centre of his silver tray. He had learned quickly that the customer is always right—who was he to question such an odd request? Much is forgiven the Fijian waiter, for he is the cheeriest, most well-meaning and obliging in the world. A broad white smile and a Hibiscus behind the ear make up for a multitude of sins. If your broad-shouldered, bare-footed table attendant happens to spill the soup down your shirtfront before doubling up with delighted laughter over his own clumsiness, what can you do but join in? The unimpeachable waiter of Continental reputation has no place here.

Tourism has wrought great change, too, among the easy-going island musicians, accustomed to singing and plucking a guitar for purely personal enjoyment. Their unschooled voices are richly versatile, evocative of romance and sensual pleasure. They sing of love and adventure, recording the history of generations

and recalling long nights around the grog bowl in the time when such entertainments as movie theatres and radio were beyond comprehension. With hotels and tourists has come a new field of entertainment—and not just for pleasure. Scores of new young singers, dancers and musicians have emerged, hopeful of sharing in the limelight. There are material rewards now for doing what they love most—and even if they feel a certain apathy regarding hard work and competition, they are bent on proving that Fiji doesn't need second-rate acts from overseas.

The entertainment scene isn't slick or sophisticated . . . it's ebullient, unpredictable, colourful, enjoyable, which makes it authentically South Seas in character. On various nights around Viti Levu a visitor might regale himself of full-scale meke entertainment staged by ceremonially-garbed Fijian groups, or listen a bit to the frenetic sounds of weirdly-named bands intent on satisfying the ear-splitting demands of the young. He might observe a muscular young man in mini-sarong performing the heart-stopping Samoan knife and fire dance, or cast

a speculative eye on the twitching hips of a slim brown tamoure dancer. He will see all this, sample the comforts of well-appointed hotels, browse in air-conditioned shops, travel by air-conditioned coach. He might visit a village or two and speak with the people in the market-place, but even so — if he's the average visitor—he'll be seeing only the facade of Fiji, the superficial gloss imposed by the accoutrements of progress.

Away from the towns, with their hotels and increasingly competitive industrial and commercial develop-

ment, the mass of Fijians and Indians still live much as they were living two or three decades ago and think, perhaps, only a little differently. The thin veneer of sophistication seems to be just that—a veneer. Beneath it, both Fijians and Indians adhere to their customs and revere their ancient traditions with the safe knowledge that many other generations before them have done the same, protected against the shifting whims of the outside world. Some of the younger ones have adopted Western custom with a zest that is often misdirected. You see them, favouring attitudes and clothes in grotesque imitation of favourite movie heroes, mooching on street corners in their high-heeled boots, swooping through the sleepy suburbs in motorcycle gangs. But theirs, too, is a facade, for they haven't the conditioned toughness of the true hooligan or child of the slums. It is a garment to be shed whenever it is time to return to the village or the bosom of the family.

The intrusion of a money economy on what was largely a coconut cash subsistence economy has brought its problems, but in many of the villages of the interior and in the outer islands, where only a little wealth filters through, life is not too much changed since the days of the missionaries. Churches, often far bigger and grander than the chiefly bure, bear witness to the success of those who first brought the Christian message. In village life, the church is of supreme importance; if it is damaged, then the whole village will pull together to raise money for repairs. When a hurricane destroyed the church of Naqarani Village, Rewa, in 1953, the people sent thirty of their number to work in New Zea-

The Council House *(left)* and the Methodist Church *(above)* at Tubou village, Lakeba, Lau Group

land for nine months. When they had $4,000 between them, they returned home and set about rebuilding their church, each man devoting three hours every Saturday to the job. It took them a long time and most of their money—but they had their place of worship.

While they are faithful church-goers and devout Christians, there is much about Fijian thinking that the Westerner cannot understand. Inherent in the Fijian nature is a system of gaining things by begging for them from a member of the same tribe or community group—a custom quite alien to the Western and Asian concept of private property. If a Fijian approaches another with downcast eyes and a shy, sidling movement, chances are he's about to employ the 'what's yours is mine' theory. The word *kere* means to beg or ask for, and to the Western mind, which finds open-handed generosity either stupid or suspicious, the practice which has become known as *kerekere* seems almost to border on theft. This strange custom—which still exists in some parts, although it is now against the law—has ancient beginnings.

Above:
Tobacco grower, Sabeto Valley
Facing page:
Fijian Chief, Serua Island

Village elder, Naviti Island

Fisherman, Serua Island

It is said by some that when the great Serpent God Degei and Chief Lutunasobasoba came out of the west with their followers and landed at Vuda, a point jutting out into the sea along the north-west coast of Viti Levu, near Nadi's international airport, the first settlements, called *yavatu,* were founded. After his death, the spirit of each founder was known as *kalou vu* (meaning ghost, or spirit of origin) and venerated by his descendants as an 'ancestor' god who watched over the destinies of his own people. The Fijians believed it was the right of each member of a tribe to have common ownership of the property of another tribe to whom he was related, even remotely, through an ancestor god. This common-ownership custom was sacred and villagers could visit distant relatives, stay as pampered guests for as long as they wished, then leave for home, taking any goods they particularly coveted.

The *kerekere* custom has died hard. And it is one of the reasons for the difficulty these happy, sharing islanders have had adjusting to their new role as wage-earners. In the old days, wealth—in the form of a healthy harvest—wasn't to be hoarded. It had to be used or given away as quickly as possible. Now, with dollars and cents the substitute, new-found affluence is squandered in a similar way. It is the great difference between the Fijian and his individualistic Indian neighbour, who works hard and saves his money to build spacious concrete houses where several families may live, or to invest in a shop, or to send his children overseas to study medicine and law.

Fiji Police Force bandsman, Suva

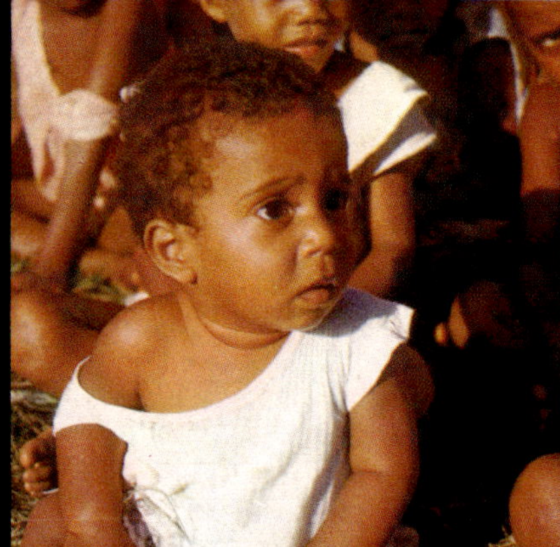

Fijian child, Vanua Levu

Above:
Chinese priest, Korolevu
Facing page:
Indian woman, Deuba

Resting before fish-drive, Serua

Yet, as in the case of the church at Naqarani, this Fijian share-all philosophy, sometimes described as the most pure, uncorrupted form of socialism in the world, becomes a force for progress when operated on a community basis. There is no need for social services in a village where children are everyone's responsibility, where old people are taken in and cared for because of a sense of 'family', rather than through obligation. If there is land to be cleared, the villagers, working all together, including women and children, will do it in a day. If there is a school to be built or bures to be repaired, many willing hands make light work of the task. Over the whole system presides the chief, who inspires almost god-like reverence. The influence of the chiefs is strong in Fijian community life and loyalty to them runs deep.

Community effort counts in every sphere, particularly the gathering of food. The tiny toy-like island of Serua, floating in reef-fringed waters off the coastline between Suva and Korolevu, is one of the best places for seeing the traditional *yavi rau,* or fish-drive, with 'scare' lines, involv-

The traditional yavi rau, or fish-drive, off
Serua Island

ing the people of a whole village, or
even two or three villages. Preparation begins a couple of days before
the tide is deemed right, with everyone helping to twist jungle vine into
a thick rope long enough to encircle
perhaps half a mile of reef. Bunches
of leaves are attached at six-foot
intervals and coconut fronds wrapped around it. A little time before the
tide reaches its height and begins
its ebb, the homespun rope—the
'scare' line—is taken by punt to the
fringing reef and played out in a
huge circle. It is an operation involv-
ing much explanation from the head

man and much light-hearted bantering among those taking part as they station themselves, chest-deep in water, around the circle.

Then, slowly and surely, they begin to shrink the enclosed area by moving towards a central point, pushing the vine and its trailing coconut fronds before them, to the accompaniment of high-spirited shouting and splashing. The captive fish are herded together into shallow pools and as the tide ebbs to its lowest point, hundreds and hundreds of fish are exposed, This is the moment of real excitement, with everybody shouting at once and the fish churning the water until it resembles a boiling cauldron. Then, with shouts of glee, the villagers begin spearing their catch with home-made harpoons and sharpened sticks, thrusting into water turned murky and slightly pink and filling the punts in a matter of minutes. In the early days this ingenious method of 'driving' fish enabled Fijian fishermen to reap huge harvests from the sea. Even today, it sometimes seems quite as effective as more modern and far less spectacular methods.

The harvest from the sea

History and tradition

Cross on Taveuni hills seen from a ship passing through the Somosomo Strait

It can be seen for miles, this massive cross glowing whitely against the thickly-wooded backdrop of the Taveuni hills. Sixty feet tall and made of cement, it was raised in 1964 to replace another less permanent one which had rotted away after standing for half a century. It is the monument of the Mission of the Holy Cross, Wairiki, a constant reminder of the dedicated labours of not only the Roman Catholic, but all the missionaries who came to Fiji and set it on a new path in history. Although less than fifteen per cent of Fijians are Roman Catholics— more than eighty per cent of them are Methodists—this particular cross and its nearby church of coral stone and cement, with stained glass windows brought from France and simple grass mats instead of pews, have a special place in that history. They mark the turning point of resistance among the people of Cakaudrove (which includes Taveuni) against missionaries, and Roman Catholic missionaries in particular.

It was here, in July 1862, that a famous war against Tongan invaders
was waged and won in a single day
by Fijian chiefs and warriors. They
carried small crosses presented to
them by the Reverend Father Loresio
Favre, who until then had been having a hard time sowing the seed of
Catholicism in the region. The
priest promised the Fijians that they
need have no fear while they carried
the crosses . . . and after the defeat
of the Tongans, the Fijian leader,
Ratu Golea, prized his crucifix as the
cross of victory, vowing there and
then that he and his men would be-

Pottery making, the oldest Fijian craft,
survives near Sigatoka

come Catholics. There was nothing Christian about the battle itself however, for it ended with the triumphant Fijians tearing the livers and hearts out of some of their victims—an action not at all unusual in the islands then known far and wide as the Cannibal Isles.

The fearsome title was well earned; there are many authenticated tales about the bloodthirsty activities of the chiefs and their warriors. The most frequently related is that of the ill-fated Wesleyan, who was destined to become known as the last white missionary to fall victim to Fijian cannibalism. He was the Reverend Thomas Baker, slain with a battle-axe on 20 July 1867 and then eaten, boots and all. There is the tale, too, of Udreudre, of the prodigious appetite. His passion for human flesh was said to be such that he managed to eat some 900 bodies during his life! A stone monument observing his effort can be seen by the roadside in the district of Rakiraki, where he was chief. Historians tell of feasts where hundreds of bodies were served up and eaten— with the hearts and tongues considered the delicacies. But while much was made during those times of the 'debased savagery' of these fine-physiqued warriors, with their proud, almost arrogant bearing and massive heads of hair, many writers paid tribute to the kindness and affection shown by some of the cannibals towards their white friends. It is certainly still true that when not engaged in warfare (their prowess as unbeatable guerrilla fighters was seen during World War II in the Pacific), Fijians exhibit a mildness and open-handed generosity quite alien to most other races.

ER
FIJI POLICE
SALUS POPULI

Bula Festival, Nadi

Previous page:
Changing the guard at Government House,
Suva. The Fiji Military Forces (*left*) and
the Fiji Police Force

Their wide, warm smiles may mask a history of violence and tumult, but they do so very effectively.

Until firearms were introduced to Fiji by European adventurers at the beginning of the 19th century, local weapons were restricted to elaborately carved spears, clubs and bows and arrows. To defend mountain strongholds, Fijian warriors would surprise their enemies by raining huge boulders down upon them; slings were used to hurl stones with enormous force and accuracy. The first musket came with the wreck of the brig *Eliza* on the Mocea reef in 1808, and the subsequent arrival on Bau of one of the survivors, the disreputable Charlie Savage, who attached himself to the chief and taught the Bauans how to use the awesome thunder-producing weapons of the *vavalagi.*

But white intruders had first appeared long before—as far back as 1643, when the Dutchman, Abel Tasman, sighted the Nanuku passage and a dozen islands, but failed to land. Almost a century and a half later, Bligh sighted and charted thirty-nine islands, of which the main island, Viti Levu, was one. The first of his two Fiji journeys was made in an open launch, following the famous mutiny on the *Bounty*; it was a trip made under appalling conditions and lasting for 3,600 miles. Bligh came again in 1792, this time in the warship HMS *Providence*, and he added to the discoveries he'd made during his first astounding voyage. That other great Pacific adventurer, Captain James Cook, is credited with the first sighting of Vatoa, one of the small southern Lau islands. Captain James Wilson, of the London missionary ship *Duff* discovered many of the islands

Sunset on Suva Harbour

and reefs of the northern part of Lau. However, these 18th century discoveries made little initial impact on a culture and society which recent finds indicate may date back as far as 1290 BC The earliest white settlers were survivors of shipwrecks and although they became popular as prestigious tribal acquisitions, they did little to change the face of chiefly and tribal politics. But then came the sandalwood seekers. They sailed their ships to the west coast of Vanua Levu and began a thriving trade in timber, paving the way for those who later began trading in beche-de-mer, turtle oil, coconut oil and arrowroot. It was these traders and the early missionaries who were to change Fiji.

As well as the Christian religion and new and bewildering concepts of commerce and currency, Europeans brought much that must have made the Fijians wonder whether 'civilisation' was such an enviable state. With the ships came disease. Although considered trivial by the relatively-immune European, to the Fijian such afflictions as measles and whooping cough were horrifying and frequently fatal. In 1875 an

Preparation of yaqona or kava for the traditional Fijian ceremony of welcome at the Kese village on Naviti Island, Yasawa Group.

Next pages:
The yaqona root is crushed and mixed with water

epidemic of measles caused fearful ravages among the islanders and the newly-begun *Fiji Times* ran reports of streets traversed by 'natives carrying coffins' and of 'a scourge' that caused villagers to burn down their homes and flee in utmost terror. Many thousands of Fijians died in this and other epidemics. Alcohol was another *vavalagi* wonder, which often had equally disastrous results. The old capital of Levuka, on the island of Ovalau, was packed with hotels and every second store sold alcohol. It was at Levuka on 10 October 1874 that the Deed ceding Fiji to Great Britain was signed by Cakobau, King of Fiji, Ma'afu, the Tongan Chief of Lau, eleven Fiji chiefs and, on behalf of the British Crown, Sir Hercules Robinson, Governor of the Australian State of New South Wales.

For almost a century after Fiji's voluntary entry into what was then the British Empire, the spirit of progress was Colonial. Even today, in remote villages on remote islands, photographs of every member of the British Royal family since Queen Victoria and her consort, Albert, can be seen decorating spartan bure walls. And although on 10 October 1970, Fiji chose to move outside the umbrella of British Colonialism to become independent within the Commonwealth, loyalty to the Crown was reaffirmed in the Constitution. Affection and respect for the Royal Family remains strong in the hearts and minds of the people, as does their faith in the leadership of their chiefs. Some of the early buildings remaining in Suva have a kind of seedy nostalgia, a reminder of the Empire on which it became inevitable that the tropic sun must set. It pervades the squat, grey bulk of the

The kava is offered to the guest of honour
at the century-old ceremony

Next pages:
The uniquely Fijian firewalking of the
Sawau tribesmen from Beqa Island. In spite
of the intense heat of the stones the walkers
have no scars or blisters on their feet

old Government Buildings, where once indefatigably British servants of the Colonial Office sat in pokey cupboard-sized offices, inadequately cooled by ceiling fans and surrounded by dusty files and papers. A programme of localisation has since replaced these expatriates with Fijian and Indian workers who now fill all but a handful of positions from the highest echelons of Government right down through the ranks.

It was the Colonial administration that brought Indians to Fiji, under an indenture system which lasted forty years and brought 63,000 people to work on farms and plantations. The first of them arrived in the sailing ship *Leonidas* at Levuka in 1879. The *Fiji Times* carried a cryptic report on the condition of these unfortunate first immigrants: 'As soon as communication was made with the ship, it was ascertained that cholera had been on board together with smallpox and that eleven coolies had died of cholera and six of dysentery; cholera seeming to predominate, while little seems to be known of smallpox.' The medical officer of the day devised an ingenious method of preventing contagion. He had a staging erected on the outer reef so that stores could be placed on the platform at low tide and taken off by the ship's boat. The whole staging was then demolished and allowed to float until the next low tide, when it was re-erected. All letters were placed in a carbolic acid bottle which was fumigated before delivery. The newspaper observed that: 'Communication with the vessel is of course slow but from what we learn there are 373 male and 149 female coolies on board, independent of children. . .'

In 1882 Suva was chosen as an alternative capital to Levuka and the Colony's government moved there lock, stock and barrel—not without protest from the populace. The *Fiji Times,* with its headquarters at Levuka, described the chosen site as an area of 'fetid and pestiferous marshes' and bemoaned the 'general insalubrity of the situation'. With typical verbal meanderings, the newspaper continued to lament the need to move to a place where 'shut out from the sea breeze by their own tortuous winding, the byways of this rookery appear as though specially designed to retain the malarious exhalations which continually arise from these mephitic swamps . . .' However, the move was made and Suva became the crossroads of the South Pacific.

Although Fiji has embraced 20th century sophistication, happily in some areas there remains much that is brooding and mysterious. As recently as 1969 the Legislative Council made it an offence for any race in Fiji to practise witchcraft. Discovery and prosecution now bring a lengthy prison term, so little new evidence of sorcery comes to light these days. Nevertheless, the belief in witchery and devil deeds is unshakeably strong in the minds of both islanders and Indians and weird, hair-raising stories are told around the 'grog' or yaqona bowl. The practice of *drau-ni-kau* (sorcery with leaves) has not died completely, but contracted to remoter areas and gone underground. There is 'good' magic—the healing powers of certain barks and herbs, for instance—and 'bad' magic, which comes complete with evil spells, death-dealing herbs, the puncturing of dead bodies and

sinister incantations.

Drau-ni-kau has a long history among the Melanesian and Micronesian people and it can be employed for all manner of purposes—from securing a wife, to ruining a neighbour's crop of yaqona and even murder of an enemy. But it is important for the victim to be a believer and thus susceptible to the powers of this ancient sorcery. There are many tales about *drau ni kau,* and though it's hard for the outsider to find evidence of it, there are those who swear it is still practised far more widely than might be imagined. Sometimes, when nights are very still and the thumping of a distant lali drifts on the breeze, it's possible to credit these tales—but if it happens to be Sunday, the lali is probably calling the people to church! For religion and tradition go hand in hand in this country of anomaly and contrast. Indians in particular relinquish long-held customs and beliefs with reluctance; the system of arranging marriages and paying large dowries still exists and the Indian wife, wed perhaps at sixteen or seventeen, still follows in her husband's shadow, a long way from emancipation as the Western world knows it.

An Indian wedding in Fiji is a fascinating and lavish ceremony, still conducted with all the pomp and solemnity of the Old World, and Indian firewalking is an annual practice signifying the tenacity with which the South Indians, especially, have clung to the old ways. These firewalkers wear garlands of marigolds and yellow robes, representing the robes of the Mother (Maha Devi, known, too, as the Goddess Kaali or Maari), and their faces are smeared with vermilion dye and yellow

Pre-Christian priest's oil dish from Kadavu, circa 1840, exhibited in Fiji Museum

Hindu firewalkers with skewers through their cheeks prepare to walk through white-hot ashes

turmeric powder, considered by sect members to be a symbol of prosperity and of power to destroy diseases. They carry tridents, the three prongs of which are said to destroy the three demons of lust, greed and anger. They are followed by the heavy, cloying fumes of incense and the constant beat of goatskin-covered drums.

After walking to the edge of the sea, the Hindu devotees force fine skewers through their cheeks, noses, lips, arms and earlobes, so that an end protrudes on either side. Another thrusts a skewer through his forehead. There is no sign of blood or of pain—just as there is no pain when their feet touch the white-hot ashes in the fire-pit. Whilst these Hindu rites are regarded as a spiritually elevating form of penance, steeped in religious belief, the uniquely Fijian firewalking ceremony is believed by the Fijians themselves to have legendary origin. Some Western anthropologists consider it to have definite links with ancient Asia, possibly through the travels of a Bronze Age tribe called Sora or Savara, said to be descended from the Indus people. Perhaps it was the Spirit God and the warrior called Tui-na-iviqalita who brought the gift of walking on hot stones to the Sawau tribesmen of Fiji's Beqa Island—or perhaps the secret is buried in the Bronze Age. Whatever the answer, it is true that only those who believe can survive the heat unscathed.

Left:
Fijian Rugby is always colourful and
exciting

Right:
The 2nd Battalion Fiji Military Forces

Next pages:
Building a traditional Fijian house, a bure,
using magimagi, coconut fibres, instead of
nails

Flora

In the mountain forests surrounding the crater lake on Taveuni, where mists hover almost permanently above extinct volcanic craters and the vegetation is thick and moistly-lush, there grows a flower considered by many to be the most interesting and beautiful in Fiji. It is the Tagimaucia (pronounced Tangi-mauthia), which means 'Crying in Vain'. The name originated from a mysterious legend about a child prince who lived in a mountain village believed once to have existed on Taveuni. The village has disappeared and the origin of the legend vanished into obscurity, but the fuchsia-like Tagimaucia continues to create a riot of brilliant crimson amid the sombre green of the high Taveuni jungle.

For many years people believed it to be an extremely rare orchid found only by the crater lake and the misconception lives on. But specimens have been found high up on Mt Soatura on Vanua Levu, and the unglamorous fact is that it belongs to the plant family *Melastomaceae,* a native of South America, which includes one of the worst plant pests in Fiji, *Clidemia hirta.* Nevertheless the spectacular Tagimaucia, albeit cousin to the 'curse' of the grazing land, continues to wield its fascination for botanists and all who have heard the legend.

Few tourists have seen it, of course, for it requires an excursion into the solemn gloom of jungle made thick and inhospitable by a rainfall exceeding 250 inches a year, and a climb into mountains rising just over 4,000 feet. But there's no need to venture as far as that to view the splendour of Fiji's more common flora, whether wild or cultivated, indigenous or introduced. Even in

Flowers are found in exotic abundance
everywhere in the Fiji Islands

Suva itself, you'll see a profusion of jungle growth constantly threatening to encroach upon the luxuriant gardens and tailored parklands. From November to January the branches of the stately Flamboyante, known, too, as the Poinciana, are aflame with vivid blooms, arching over Suva's avenues in a molten floral canopy. By the sides of the roads, in public parks and private gardens, the purple mass of Bougainvillea blends with the buttery blooms of sprawling Golden Allamanda vines. The permanently-coloured leaves of Croton shrubs

throw splashes of red, pink, orange and golden-bronze along the roadside and the immense pendant branches of the Golden Shower explode in a burst of feathery sunshine.

The towering African Tulip is crowned year-round with fiery masses of close-packed blossoms; Hibiscus bushes bloom in every garden and the faintly sensual perfume of the creamy-white Frangipani grows stronger as night cools the air.

There are approximately 3,000 species of plants in Fiji, just over a third of them indigenous. The most exotic and enchanting of them—the orchid—boasts more than 120 native species, the most common being the ground orchid, daintily swaying at the tip of its long slender stem in varying hues of pink and cyclamen. Its botanical name, *Spathoglottis pacifica,* does little to convey its gentle mystique. Another frequently seen Fiji orchid is the yellow and brown Dendrobium Tokai, which grows widely in the Tailevu area of Viti Levu.

Then there are the Fiji fruits including Kavika, a little round reddish-coloured fruit with a rose petal flavour; Wi, a tart-tasting green fruit which can grow to the size of a small mango; Ivi, or Tahitian Chestnut, which actually tastes like a chestnut when roasted; and, staple food in all the islands, the breadfruit, which when cooked tastes more like sweet potato than bread.

But the real symbol of the South Seas is the ubiquitous coconut palm, its long trunk standing tall or bent at crazy angles, its fringed topknot ruffling gently in the tradewinds or whipping furiously in some tropic tempest. For more generations than we can count the coconut palm has

Lush growth Savusavu, Vanua Levu

helped to shelter and feed the people of the islands, and today, still, the export of coconut products —oil, copra and meal—is one of Fiji's most important industries.

Think of the stagnant slime of mangrove swamps, dark depths of tropical jungle, rivers flowing warm and murky, and you'll probably think of crocodiles. But there are none to be found in Fiji, just as there were no bears or lions or wolves for the early European settlers to battle with—it was the human inhabitants they feared! While plant life flourishes in an abundance of species and sub-species, there is an amazing scarcity of animal wild life in the jungles and forests of these islands. Apart from several varieties of snake, none particularly fearsome; an indigenous rat and a flying-fox; some sixty-eight species of land and freshwater birds; the mongoose; great colonies of giant and miniscule toads; multitudes of land crabs; the rhinosceros beetle, scourge of the coconut palm; and the usual domestic and farm animals, there are few creatures to challenge man's presence. Among the few real pests now is the mongoose. Brought here from India in the 1880s to clean out rat-infested cane fields, the stoat-like animal fulfilled its task—then set about plundering poultry runs and native birds. Despite sporadic eradication campaigns the speedy little animal has been a pest in Fiji for three-quarters of a century.

Among the birds, nine of the sixty-eight species were brought here by outsiders, some of whom spared little thought for the future. These avian immigrants include the aggressive, omnipresent mynahs, introduced from India about 1800. Arrogant creatures, with raucous cries and bullying tactics, the mynahs have frightened the smaller native birds deep into the forests. Unfortunately, these far from endearing newcomers are extremely numerous now and look like becoming a permanent fixture. The European starling, its black feathers gleaming with a dull metallic sheen, is another notorious pest, believed to have been introduced accidentally from a passing ship. Equally destructive is the Malay Turtle Dove which consumes large quantities of grain; but at least this feathered immigrant has a pleasing voice—a soft cooing call—and a gentle look.

Most of Fiji's bird life is centred around half a dozen of the larger, wooded islands, though the Lau Group boasts three species—the Blue Crowned Lory, the Versicolor Flycatcher and the aforementioned European starling—not found anywhere else. In the country areas, exotic birds like the Red-headed Parrot Finch (the Fijians call it Kula-lailai) and the purple-crowned Collared Lory (Kula) gather in small flocks, feeding on grass seeds and small grain and rising into the air in vivid clouds of emerald, scarlet and turquoise. The islands of Koro, Gau, Kadavu and Taveuni each have a sub-species of parrot peculiar to that area, the Taveuni parrot in particular having been much prized at one time for its maroon feathers. Principal birds in the archipelago are the Island Thrush, Golden Whistler, Fiji Shrikebill, Spotted Fantail, Wattled Honeyeater, Polynesian Triller, Musk Parrot and White-collared Fantail, but it takes the experienced bird-watcher to seek them out. With the mynahs, tourism and industrial development having taken over much of the coastal area of Viti Levu, Fiji's birds have discovered less frequented haunts of their own.

Marine Life

Anchored off Castaway Island, the 84 ft
schooner *Fitheach Ban*, locally known as
'Seaspray'

On land, man may hold his own; even call the tune. Beneath the surface of the sea he is only an observer, barely tolerated in a world created over aeons for the amusement of nature and the benefit of the strange, often beautiful, often nightmarish creatures that reign there. What colour. What peace. Even the predators commit their carnage in silence. The Fiji reefs shelter gardens a thousand times more fascinating than those on land, gardens of living coral in every delicate and brilliant hue. Profusely branched staghorn corals seem to have been dipped in vivid dyes, so that the tip of each branchlet glows blue and lavender and pink. Great masses of brain coral give an impression of inexorable pulsation. Columns of fish drift by, shadowed by a cruising shark, while monster animal flowers—the giant anemones—bloom red and green and iridescent orange from small crevices, then fold into themselves and disappear. Bright blue patches of coral dot the surface of the flats, matching the intensely blue starfish and the electric blue of tiny reef fish. The sharp scalloped edges of giant clams gape open to trap the unwary. Crabs with patterned armour scuttle and sidle. An occasional octopus clithers multi-legged out of sight while a zebra-coloured sea snake undulates in the shallows.

Here, visibility in the crystal clear water is 100 ft or more, an unimpeded view of one of the largest collections of undersea life in the world. These warm waters harbour as many dangerous, even deadly creatures as any tropical ocean—and some of the most beautiful of them are also the most treacherous. The sleek grace of the black and white

Sea Turtle caught near Korolevu

Outrigger canoes, still used in the Lau Group, are becoming rare near the main islands. They are, however, being built in small numbers for the use of tourists on Viti Levu

sea snake, the dadakulaci, cloaks venom more deadly than the Indian cobra. Yet the snake is a children's plaything in Fiji and has long been believed to be completely harmless. The fact that there is no record of anyone having been bitten adds to the myth, but experiments indicate that the dadakulaci, which once infested many of the small islands around Viti Levu, is best left well alone. The gently flowing 'wings' of the lion fish make it one of the most graceful of the sea's creatures—yet its spines can pierce the skin and cause intense pain. Shells, too, can be deceptive, especially certain varieties of the exquisitely patterned cone family. Humping its shell about on a single muscle, or foot, the snail inside is capable of ejecting a tiny barbed dart, complete with poison sac. The venom can be lethal for humans and the more usual enemies of this ingenious shellfish. Not all of the hundreds of species of cones are deadly; some are considered highly palatable by the islanders.

Perhaps the most uninteresting yet sought-after product of the reef is the beche-de-mer or sea cucumber, a featureless sausage-shaped crea-ture which represented almost £18,000 to Fiji's export trade back in 1920. That was a boom year for beche-de-mer, but the tough, almost tasteless seafood is still popular with the Chinese and Japanese as well as with the Fijians. To the Chinese it is not considered an aristocratic dish like bird's nest, shark's fin or eel tripe soup, but it is sufficiently popular to have been one of Fiji's main export items for much of the first half of this century. Among the real island delicacies—rarer than caviar but with a similar specialised taste that, once ac-

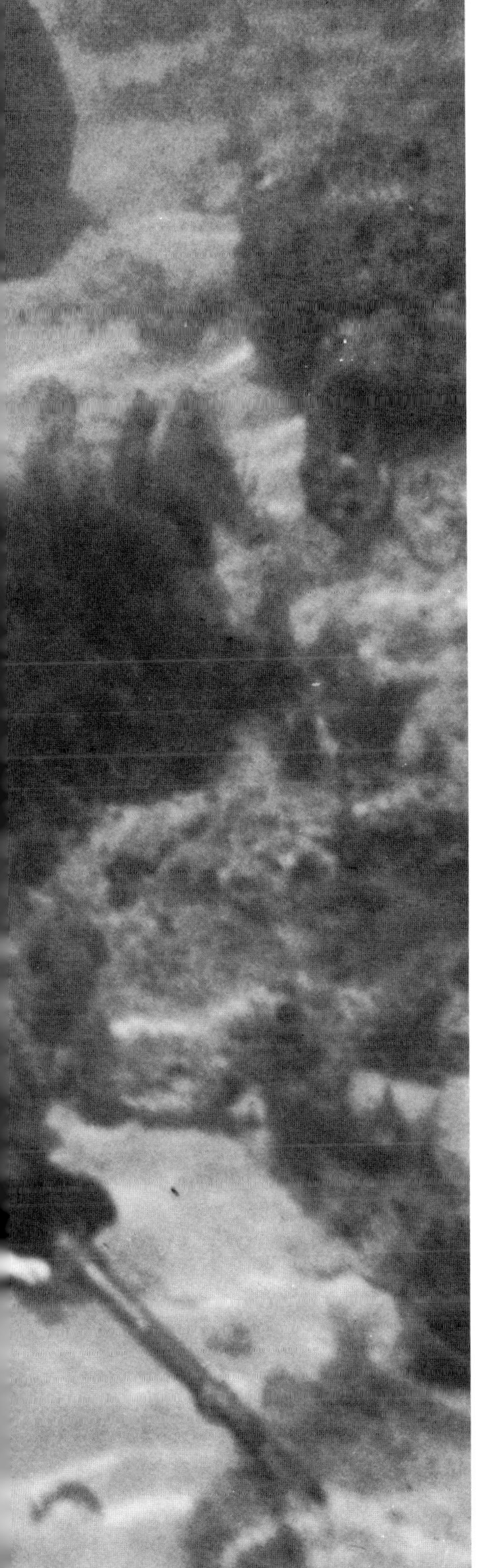

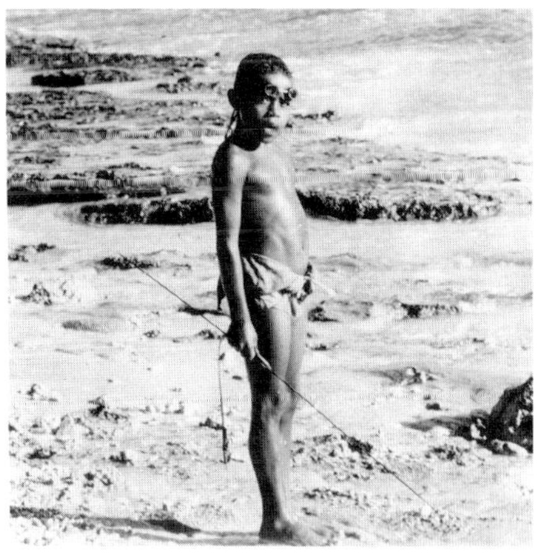

Fijian children become expert with a fish spear at a very early age, but for serious undersea hunting the modern spear gun is now used *(left and previous page)*

quired, addicts one for life—is the balolo, one of the great curiosities of the South Pacific. The rising of the balolo is an annual occurrence in several parts of Fiji, a mass migration to the surface by millions upon millions of writhing, worm-like objects that are in fact the sperm and egg sacs of the male and female sea annelid, *Palolo viridis*. A 19th century chronicler likened the balolo to a foot and a half of living vermicelli, with a mouth but no head, a transparent pipe but no body. It is believed that nothing, not even a hurricane, can prevent the rising of the balolo on two fixed nights a year. The mass upward exodus coincides with the last quarters of the moon, at a time when the sun is at its zenith, always late October or November.

A collection of local shells on display at
Fiji Museum and *(right)* the spine-covered,
coral-killing Crown of Thorns starfish,
photographed by Captain Stanley Brown on
a reef in the Koro Sea

History of the Fiji Post Office

There were many ingenious methods of communication in Fiji before the arrival of outsiders, but the first recorded use of the post was a letter carried from King George of Tonga to Tui Nayau by the Sydney schooner *Blackbird,* which arrived at Lakeba, in the Lau Group, in October 1835.

Although mail was exchanged by canoes and other craft plying between mission stations and between Tonga and Fiji, it was not until 1870 that the proprietors of the *Fiji Times* established an independent and efficient letter and parcel service centred at Levuka. There were agencies in several places, including Suva, Kadavu and Somosomo.

This service saw the introduction of the *Fiji Times* Express stamps. Quite valuable today, they were printed by letterpress and featured a rather austere design.

The well organised *Fiji Times* Express service was not appreciated by the Consul of the time, who, in 1871, endeavoured to suppress it by appointing an official Postmaster. The latter caused much dissatisfaction by charging an additional 3d per letter above the *Fiji Times* tariff in order to pay his salary.

An official postal system was set up later that year and in 1872 the Cakobau government issued its own stamps printed at the Government Printing Office in Sydney and featuring the 'CR' (Cakobau Rex) monogram. The *Fiji Times* Express was discontinued in May 1872.

With Cession in 1874, the Colonial Government took over the administration of the Post Office and in 1882 the General Post Office was established in Suva when the seat of Government was moved there.

By 1890 thirty-six postal districts had

been established and the Colonial Postmaster, Mr L. J. Walker, issued a Postal Notice requesting that the public discontinue addressing correspondence to 'Native Villages' as it was difficult to deliver them correctly. One of the reasons for correspondence going astray at this time might have been because only three of the country postmasters received any pay—one £5, another £10 and the third £15.

The introduction in 1938 of the Empire Air Mail Scheme, via Australia, was a major postal event, since, prior to that, it was usually as quick to send European mail by sea, by transferring the mail from the Pacific to the Atlantic overland through the United States.

By 1938, internal mail services had been established to all parts of Fiji—though it took rather a long time to get to some of the outlying areas. With the introduction in 1951 of regular daily Fiji Airways flights to Nadi and Vanua Lovu the mail services received the stamp of speed and efficiency. The airline, with its much expanded network, now carries well over 20,000 bags of mail a year. Twice as much again is carried by road. Fiji Airways now carries the mail to Tonga, the New Hebrides, Solomon Islands, Papua-New Guinea, Western Samoa, Gilbert and Ellice Islands and the smallest independent Republic in the world, Nauru. Quite a change from the early days when mail was delivered by canoe.

fiji
REEF FISH
Heniochus
5c

fiji
HAWK MOTH
Psilogramma Jordana
4c

fiji
BELO
REEF HERON
fiji
3c

fiji
TAKIA
ROYAL VISIT
1970
25c

fiji
160°
PACIFIC OCEAN
CAROLINE IS.
GILBERT IS.
SOLOMON IS.
TOKELAU IS.
SAMOA IS.
NEW HEBRIDES
FIJI IS.
COOK IS.
TONGA IS.
2 CENTS
INAUGURATION OF THE UNIVERSITY OF THE SOUTH PACIFIC

fiji
SOUTH PACIFIC GAMES
20c
3rd SOUTH PACIFIC GAMES 1969

fiji
50c
ORCHIDS Arundina Bambusifolia

fiji
2c
Nautilus Pompilius

fiji
BLACK MARLIN
10c

fiji
8c
3rd SOUTH PACIFIC GAMES 1969

fiji
BAMBOO RAFT
8c

NATIVE GOLD
MINING INDUSTRY
fiji
40c

fiji
Cypraea Aurantium
30c
GOLDEN COWRIE SHELL

SUN BIRDS
fiji
15c

25th ANNIVERSARY OF THE F.M.F. SOLOMONS
CAMPAIGN
fiji
10c
23rd June, 1944

25c
fiji
25th Anniversary of
the F.M.F. Solomons
Campaign 23rd June, 1944.

TABUA
fiji
$1

fiji
PASSION FRUIT FLOWER
1c

25th ANNIVERSARY OF THE F.M.F.
SOLOMONS CAMPAIGN 23rd June, 1944.
SOLOMON ISLANDS
fiji
3c

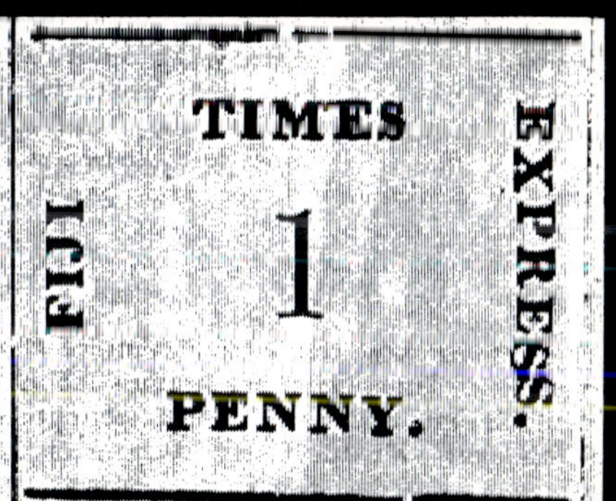

TIMES
EXPRESS.
FIJI
1
PENNY.

OPENING OF NEW GPO
SUVA
23 JA 67

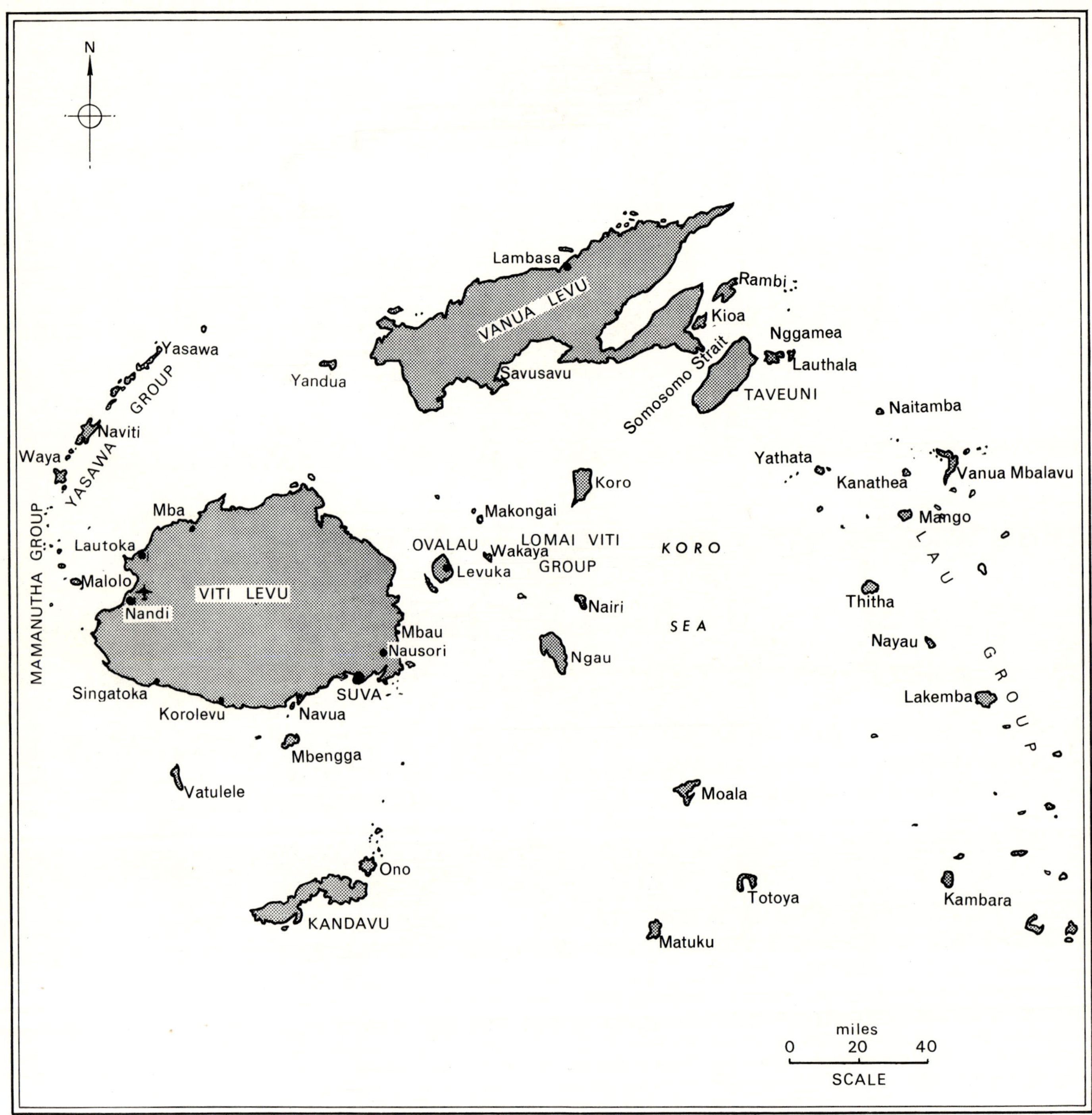

The spelling on this map is correct phonetically under the international agreement on map nomenclature.

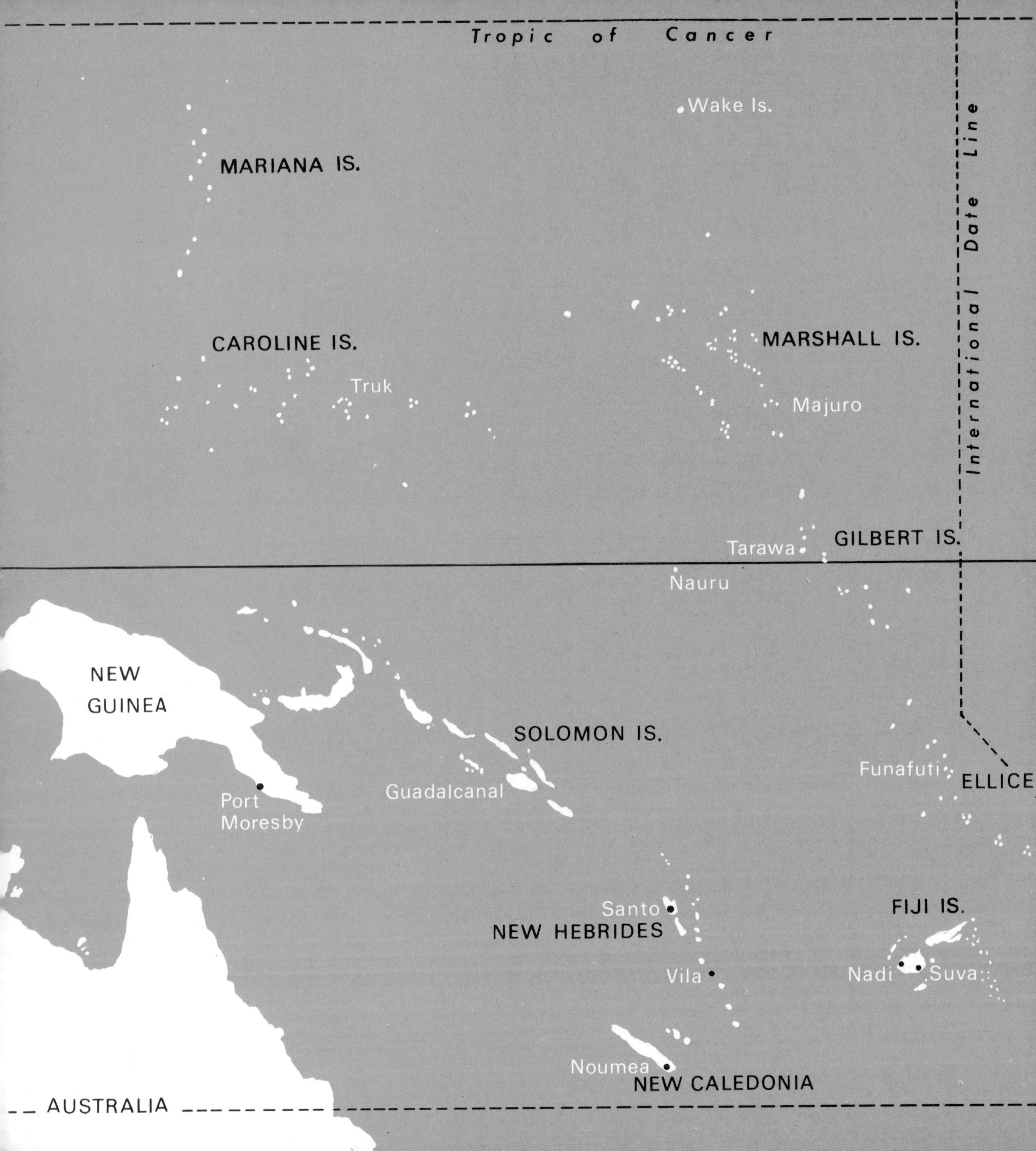

Tropic of Cancer
International Date Line
Wake Is.
MARIANA IS.
CAROLINE IS.
Truk
MARSHALL IS.
Majuro
Tarawa
GILBERT IS.
Nauru
NEW GUINEA
SOLOMON IS.
Guadalcanal
Port Moresby
Funafuti
ELLICE
Santo
NEW HEBRIDES
FIJI IS.
Vila
Nadi
Suva
Noumea
NEW CALEDONIA
AUSTRALIA